ESCAPE!

THE ENGINE ROOM

SOLVE YOUR WAY OUT!

ACCESS DENIED!

Use your **ENGINEERING** skills to **ESCAPE!**

Alix Wood

Gareth Stevens PUBLISHING

I0811253

Please visit our website, www.garethstevens.com. For a free color catalog of all our high-quality books, call toll free 1-800-542-2595 or fax 1-877-542-2596.

Cataloging-in-Publication Data
Names: Wood, Kevin.
Title: The engine room: solve your way out! / Kevin Wood.
Description: New York : Gareth Stevens, 2023. | Series: Escape!
Identifiers: ISBN 9781538277256 (pbk.) | ISBN 9781538277270 (library bound) | ISBN 9781538277263 (6 pack) | ISBN 9781538277287 (ebook)
Subjects: LCSH: Puzzles--Juvenile literature. | Problem solving--Juvenile literature. | Logic puzzles--Juvenile literature. | Engineering--Juvenile literature.
Classification: LCC GV1493.W663 2023 | DDC 793.73--dc23

Copyright © 2022 Alix Wood Books

Adaptations to North American edition © 2023
by Gareth Stevens Publishing
29 East 21st Street
New York, NY 10010

All rights reserved. No part of this book may be reproduced in any form without permission in writing from the publisher, except by a reviewer.

Produced for Gareth Stevens Publishing by Alix Wood Books
Designed and Illustrated by Alix Wood
Editor: Eloise Macgregor

Printed in the United States of America

CPSIA compliance information: Batch # CSGS23 For further information contact Gareth Stevens, New York, New York at 1-800-542-2595.

The trip to the navy base was exciting. To visit the ship, you had to go through strict security. At lunchtime, your group headed off the ship to a cafeteria. Then, you realized you had forgotten something.

You left your lunch on the ship! You quickly sneak back through the metal hatch while no one is looking. The heavy, metal door slams shut behind you. What strange symbols! You see a note stuck on the wall. Maybe that will help you open the hatch?

No key? Our ship's notebook will help you escape. Clues are everywhere!

HOW TO ESCAPE!

Use your engineering knowledge to puzzle your way out of the engine room. Solve puzzles to get the codes you need to open a series of locked boxes. Each box contains one shaped key. You need all the shapes to open the door and escape. All the information you need to solve the puzzles can be found in this book. The answer to a puzzle on one page may be found on other pages or in the notebook.

Get stuck? Answers and hints are hidden at the back of this book.

THE CORRIDOR

You wander down the corridor, looking for clues to help puzzle your way out. On the floor, among some tools, you see a locked box. The lock needs four numbers to open it. Perhaps there is a key in the box? But what are the four numbers? Could those cogs on the wall have something to do with it?

0
1
2
3
4
5
6
7
8
9
Turn the blue handle counterclockwise. Watch the cogs spin this way and that.
6

THE OFFICE

You see a light on in a room along the corridor. In the room, you find a desk covered by a muddle of maps and drawings. On the desk, there is a locked box. There are some strange shapes drawn on the lock.

Troy Island
Hay Island
Parry Island
Naval Base
Rock Island
Craggy Point
Port
Ship
N
E
S
W
10:45
STEP 7: REDESIGN THE MODEL IF IT DOESN'T WORK. THEN TEST IT AGAIN.
0 0 0

THE FLOODED HOLD

You hear what sounds like water sloshing. You go back to the corridor and head down the ladder. The cargo hold is flooding! Three boxes on planks are under the water. You could lever the boxes out of the water with the right amount of weight on the other end of each plank. There is a safe on the wall. It needs a three-digit code to open it.

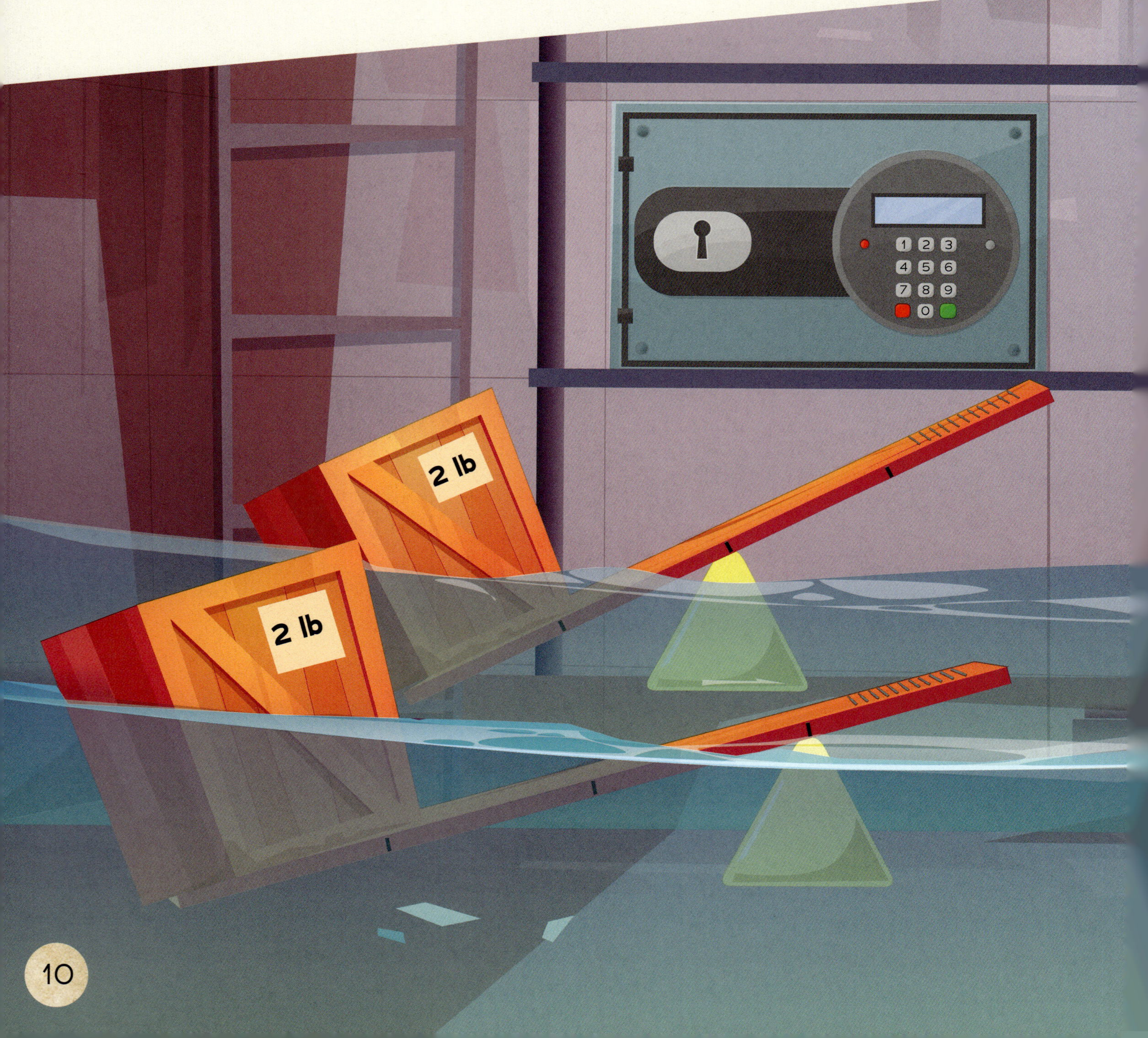

Number
7
BEST RAIL
JOURNEYS
2 lb

ENGINE ROOM

The engines are eerily silent in the still ship. In a corner of the engine room, you see a maze of pipes and numbered bottles. A locked cabinet stands on the floor. It needs a four-number code.

1
2
3
4
5
6
7
8

DRAWING OFFICE

Heading away from the damp lower decks, you come across a design room. A working dinosaur model sits on the desk, next to some plans and drawings. A ripped note is clipped to the drawing board. A locked safe sits on the floor.

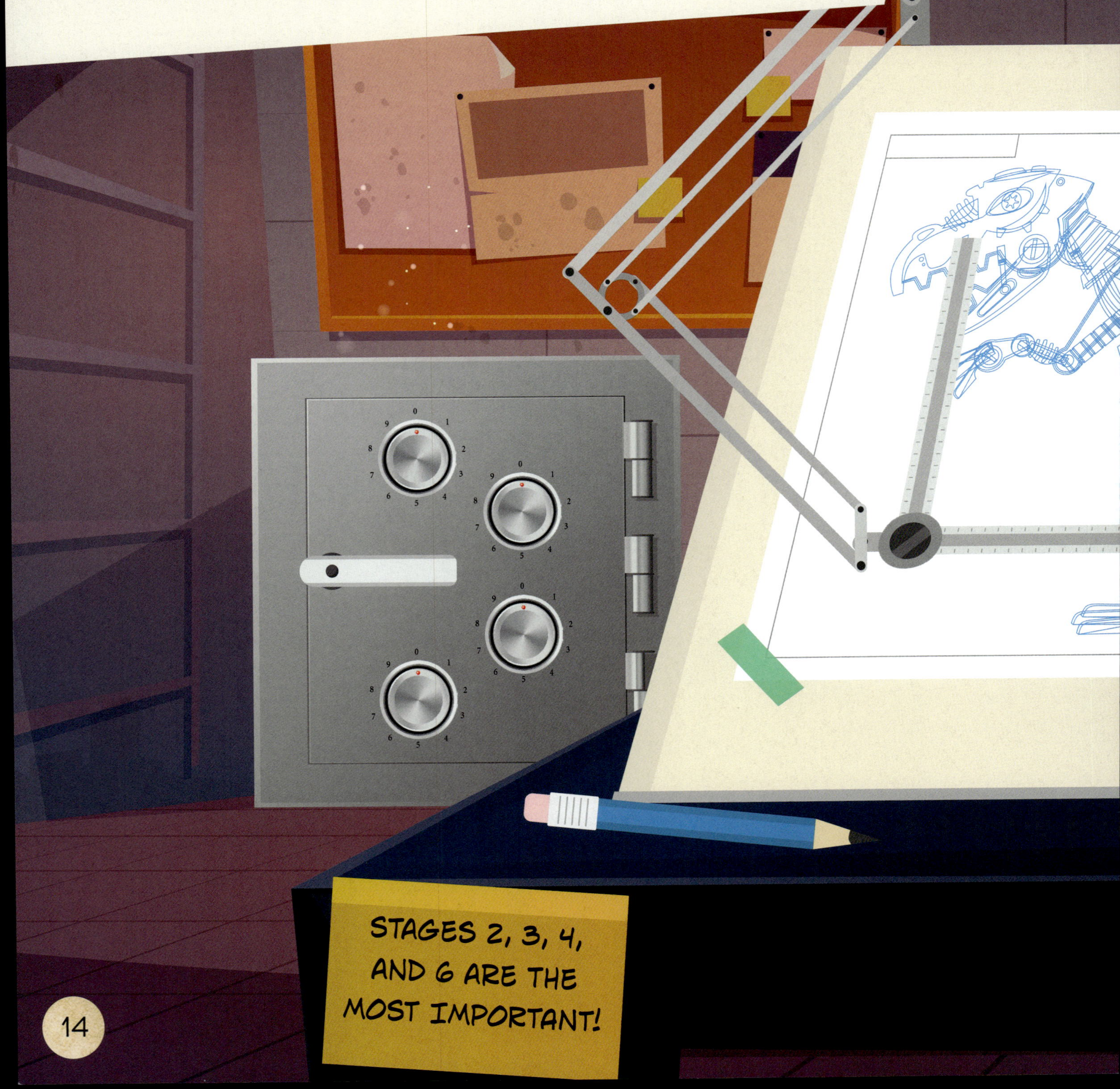

DESIGN PROCESS
STEP 1: WHAT PROBLEM SHOULD MY DESIGN SOLVE? WE NEED A REMOTE-CONTROL MODEL DINOSAUR.
STEP 2:

THE FLOOR

On the floor of the drawing office, you see an envelope. It has a strange design on the front. A notebook lies on the floor. Could that be the helpful notebook mentioned on the note by the door? I hope so!

SHIP ENGINEER'S NOTEBOOK

BAROMETERS MEASURE AIR PRESSURE. THEY HELP PREDICT THE WEATHER.

* IF THE PRESSURE IS RISING AND HIGH, THE WEATHER WILL BE FINE.
* IF THE PRESSURE IS FALLING, IT WILL BE WET, WINDY, AND GRAY.
* IF PRESSURE FALLS OR RISES QUICKLY, IT WILL BE WINDY.

AHEAD MEANS FORWARD AND ASTERN MEANS BACKWARD. FULL IS THE FASTEST SPEED.

Remember - only clockwise cogs count

SIX SIMPLE MACHINES

SIMPLE MACHINES MAKE WORK EASIER. THEY HAVE FEW OR NO MOVING PARTS. THEY WORK BY CHANGING THE DIRECTION OF A FORCE OR THE AMOUNT OF FORCE NEEDED TO DO SOMETHING.

1. A pulley has a rope and wheels. It helps pull things up. The wheel changes the direction of a force. As you pull one end of the rope down, the wheel turns and pulls the other end up.

2. A lever is a board or bar that rests on a base called a fulcrum. Levers help move heavy objects. When you push down on one side of a lever, the other side goes up. The closer the fulcrum is to the object, the easier it is to lift it.

3. A wedge helps split material. When you force the thin end of a wedge into something, its widening shape forces the object apart.

4. When a wheel rolls around a central rod, called an axle, the rolling causes less friction than if you pushed the wheels along the ground.

5. An inclined plane is a slope. It is easier to push a heavy thing up a slope than to lift it.

6. A screw is actually an inclined plane wrapped around a rod! It changes circular motion to linear motion. Screws can be used to lift things, like the screw-shaped rod in a car jack. They also can hold things together.

WEIGHT, FULCRUMS, AND LEVERS:

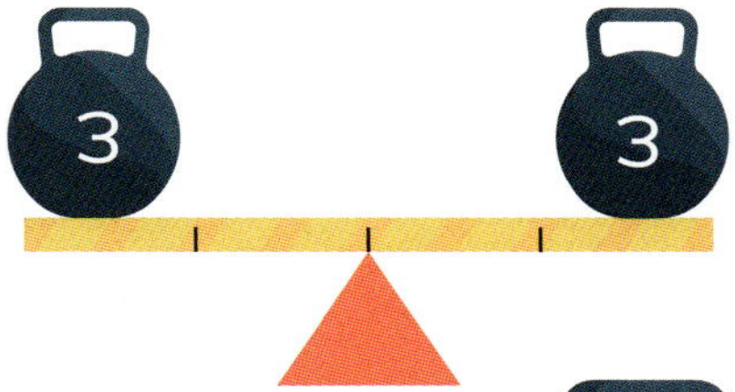

IF THE FULCRUM IS IN THE CENTER OF A 4-FOOT (OR A 4-METER) PLANK, THE SAME WEIGHT AT EACH END WILL MAKE THE PLANK LEVEL.

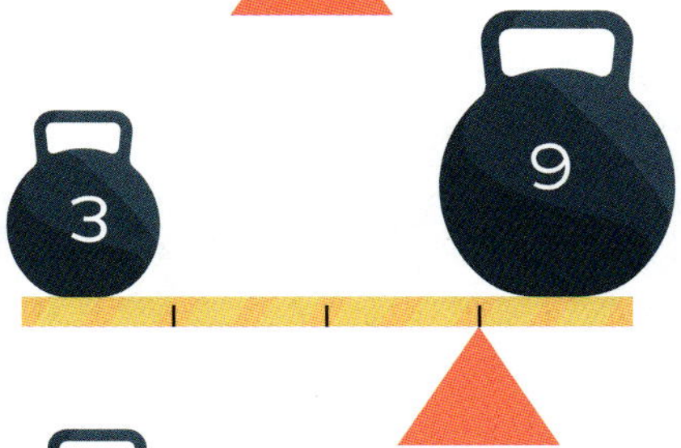

MOVE THE FULCRUM TO THE 3-FOOT MARK OF A 4-FOOT PLANK. YOU NOW HAVE A 3-FOOT LENGTH VERSUS A 1-FOOT LENGTH. YOU NEED THREE TIMES MORE WEIGHT TO MAKE THE PLANK LEVEL.

MOVE THE FULCRUM TO THE 1-FOOT MARK OF A 4-FOOT PLANK. YOU WILL NEED ONE-THIRD OF THE WEIGHT TO MAKE THE PLANK LEVEL.

IF THE FULCRUM IS AT THE 1-FOOT MARK OF A 3-FOOT PLANK, YOU HAVE A 1-FOOT LENGTH VERSUS A 2-FOOT LENGTH. THE WEIGHT NEEDS TO BE TWO TIMES BIGGER TO MAKE THE PLANK LEVEL.

TYPES OF BRIDGES

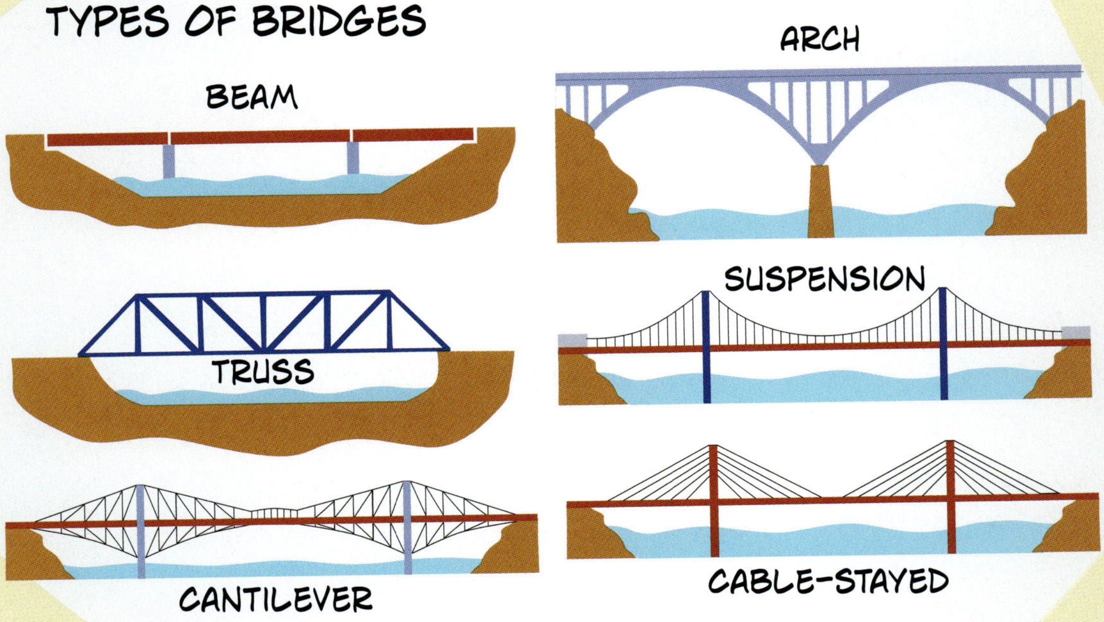

REMEMBER THE ENGINEERING DESIGN PROCESS:

STEP 1: WHAT PROBLEM DOES MY DESIGN NEED TO SOLVE?
STEP 2: RESEARCH THE PROBLEM
STEP 3: THINK UP POSSIBLE SOLUTIONS
STEP 4: SELECT A SOLUTION
STEP 5: BUILD A PROTOTYPE MODEL
STEP 6: TEST THE PROTOTYPE
STEP 7: REDESIGN IT IF I NEED TO

Engineering drawings need to be precise. An object is drawn from different views, so engineers will know exactly how to produce the object. A multi-view drawing will usually include a top view, front and side views, and a bottom view.

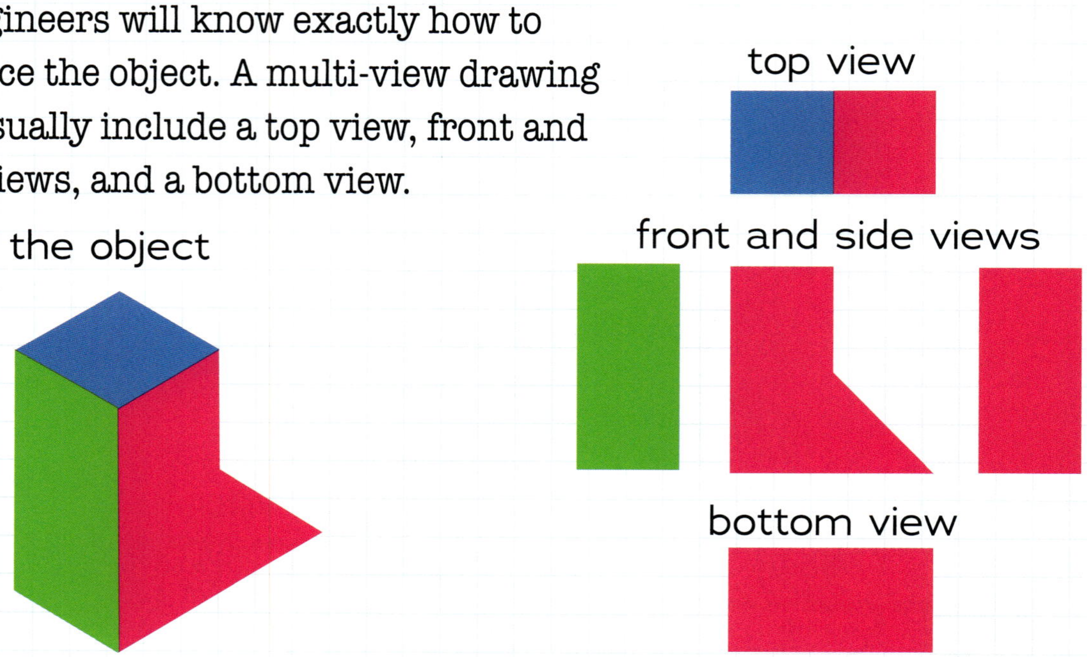

A PLUMB BOB IS A WEIGHT ON A STRING THAT IS HUNG FROM A HOOK. THE STRING HANGS PERFECTLY VERTICAL. THE VERTICAL LINE HELPS CRAFTSMEN BE SURE BUILDING WORK IS STRAIGHT. IT CAN BE USED OVER THE SIDE OF A SHIP TO MEASURE THE DEPTH OF WATER TOO. THE STRING IS MARKED EVERY FEW FEET OR METERS.

A ship's captain sends orders to the engine room using an engine order telegraph (EOT). Moving the handle on the bridge's EOT rings a bell in the engine room and moves the pointer on the engine room EOT to the same position. The engineers move their handle to match the pointer, and then follow the order.

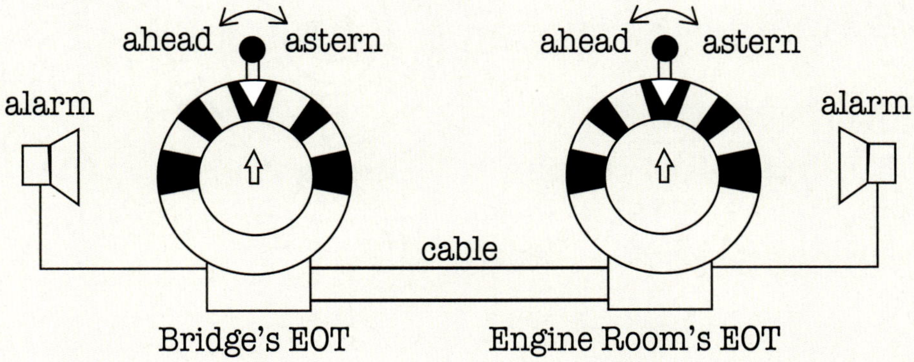

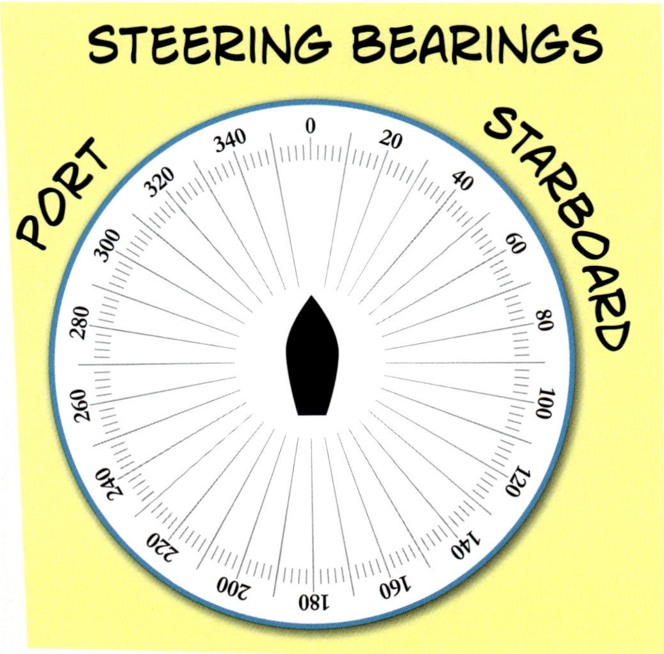

STEP 4: SELECT 1 SOLUTION.

STEERING A SHIP'S WHEEL MOVES THE RUDDER UNDER THE WATER, WHICH TURNS THE SHIP. TO HEAD LEFT (KNOWN AS "PORT"), TURN THE SHIP'S WHEEL TO THE LEFT.

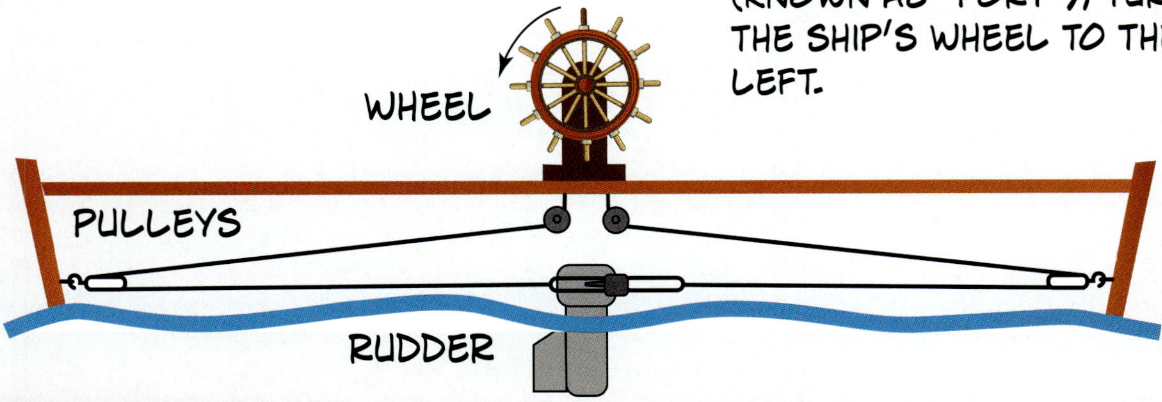

COGS AND BELTS

COGS TURN IN THE OPPOSITE DIRECTION TO THE COG BEFORE THEM.

IF TWO COGS ARE JOINED BY A BELT, THE DIRECTION WILL DEPEND ON WHETHER THE BELT IS CROSSED OR NOT.

OPPOSITE DIRECTION

SAME DIRECTION

OPPOSITE DIRECTION

RESEARCH THE PROBLEM. EXAMINE AT LEAST 3 DINOSAUR SKELETONS.

THE SHELVES

Leaving the drawing office, you pass along a corridor. A set of shelves display colorful shapes, neatly arranged in number order. Where have you seen those colors before? A wooden chest lies on the floor.

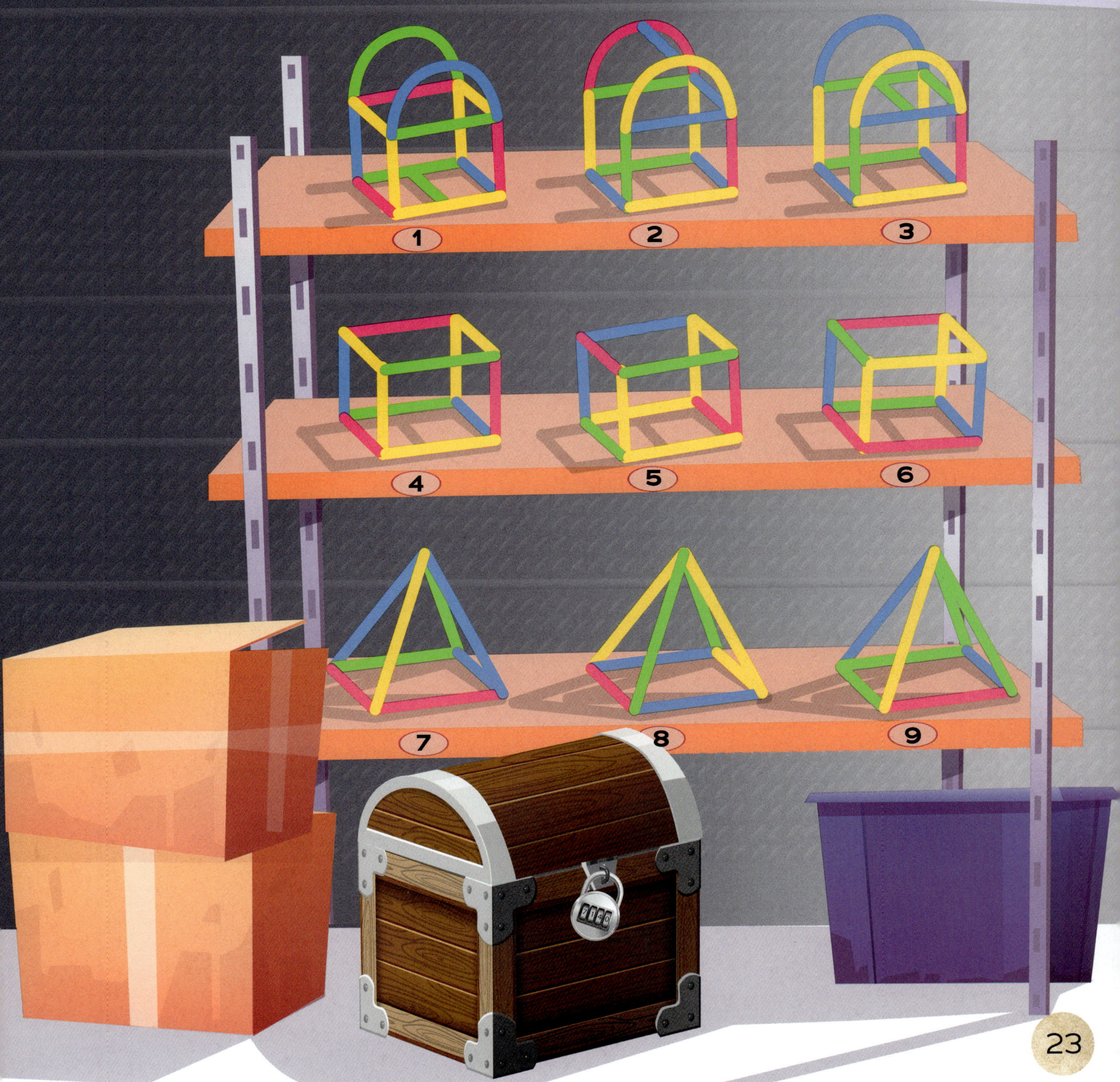

THE BUNKROOM

It seems as if someone was halfway through putting up some shelves in the bunkroom. A locked toolbox lies on the floor. It needs four numbers to open the lock. I wonder if there are any clues in this room?

What's the right tool for the job?
1 2 3 4
5 6 7 8
9 0 Enter
Clear

THE WORKSHOP

Tools everywhere! This must be a busy part of the ship since there are so many jobs to do. A padlocked toolbox lies on the metal shelf rack.

JOBS TO DO
CHOP SOME WOOD.
GET THE SACK TRUCK AND MOVE THE GAS TANKS NEXT DOOR.
JACK UP THE CART TO FIX THE WHEEL.
RAISE THE FLAG.
2 3 4 5 6 7
9 10 11 12 13 14
16 17 18 19 20
23 24 25 26 27
30 31
5

THE MAP TABLE

On a desk in the corner of the engine room, you find a map. There are some sticky labels marking some bridges on the map. A locked container sits on top of some drawings. You're sure you've seen some other bridges somewhere . . .

STEP 5: BUILD A PROTOTYPE MODEL.

THE SHIP'S BRIDGE

Dials, wheels, and screens confuse you as you enter the ship's bridge. A small blinking screen on the control desk seems to need a three-number code. But where is the safe? Out of the window, you see a storm approaching. The weather report looks bad. What direction should you steer the ship, and how fast?

Did you escape the engine room?
Check your answers on page 32.

HINTS

The Corridor
1. If only you knew how cogs worked . . .
2. What direction will each cog turn?
3. Just four numbers? Search the whole book for a clue.

The Office
1. Do the drawings on the lock resemble anything?
2. The drawing's colors look familiar. There are shapes a little like that later in the book.
3. Imagine you are a bird looking down.

The Flooded Hold
1. Some information about levers might help.
2. Make sure you know how long each plank is.
3. Find the right weights, from left to right, to lift the boxes. (The abbreviation for the weight unit called pounds is "lb.")

The Engine Room
1. What would happen if you turned on that tap?
2. There's a clue to what you need on the big pipes.
3. Water will empty out of the lowest holes first, into the bottle below.

The Drawing Office
1. Where is the rest of that ripped note?
2. Examine the steps you need to take.
3. Find the numbers hidden in the steps mentioned on the yellow sticky note.

The Shelves
1. Is that a wood chest?
2. Examine the envelope on page 16 for clues.
3. Can you find a clock that says the time?

The Bunkroom
1. What is a useful tool for getting things straight?
2. The notebook may have a clue.
3. What if you hung the tool on that hook?

The Workshop
1. Work through that to-do list!
2. If only you could find the simple machines you need . . .
3. Look closely at the tools.

The Map Table
1. What do those bridge names look like?
2. The notebook may help you.
3. Look around the book for each type of bridge.

The Ship's Bridge
1. Look at the weather map. Then find another map to work out what direction you need to steer the ship.
2. The notebook will help you work out the degrees.
3. Adjust the handle to get the right speed.

ANSWERS A mirror will help you read these answers.

6-7: 1479 [the cogs that would turn clockwise]

8-9: 385 [the top views of the arch shape, pyramid, and cube shapes on page 23; the colors on the table on page 8 help too]

10-11: 621 [the weights needed to balance the boxes, from left to right]

12-13: 6427 [the first four bottles that would fill with water, in order]

14-15: 3514 [the numbers in the description of stages 2, 3, 4, and 6]

23: 1045 [read the envelope on page 16 in the order of the colored squares—"to open the wood chest find out the time"]

24-25: 1439 [the numbers that the string would make appear if you hung the plumb bob from the hook above the wonky shelves]

26-27: 8643 [the numbers on the wedge (axe), wheel and axle (sack truck), screw (jack), and pulley (flagpole)]

28-29: 5731 [the numbers on the pictures of bridges scattered around the book]

30-31: 90 degrees and full ahead [Find your position on the map on page 9. Steer starboard 90 degrees to the good weather. Full ahead is the fastest speed]